The Chase: Trump Vs Biden

Josephs Quartzy

Published by BONGO TIMES NOW, 2024.

While every precaution has been taken in the preparation of this book, the publisher assumes no responsibility for errors or omissions, or for damages resulting from the use of the information contained herein.

THE CHASE: TRUMP VS BIDEN

First edition. March 5, 2024.

Copyright © 2024 Josephs Quartzy.

ISBN: 979-8224916733

Written by Josephs Quartzy.

Table of Contents

This mini-book is dedicated to dear friends in the United States of America.

JOSEPHS QUARTZY

THE CHASE

Table of Contents

Foreign Policies & War initiatives

My ViewPoint & Where I Stand

JOSEPHUS QUARTZY

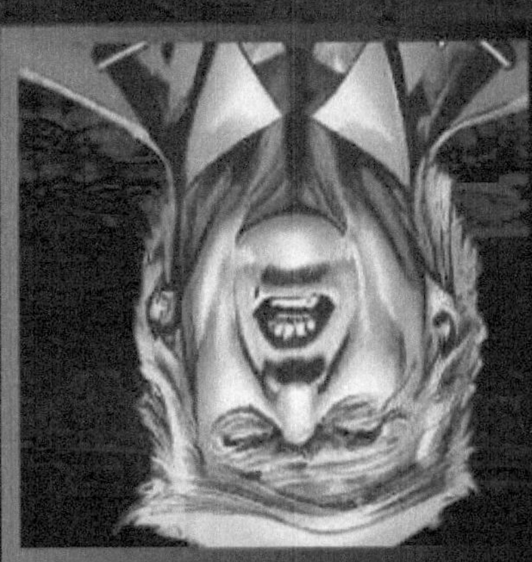

THE CHASE

Table of contents

Disclaimer

Disclaimer:

In the pages that follow, I endeavor to explore the complex narratives surrounding Donald Trump and Joe Biden. It is essential to clarify that my intent is not to align with any particular side or team, nor to advocate for or against any individual. Instead, I aim to offer a thoughtful examination based on my observations and analysis. My sole purpose is to present a comprehensive portrayal of these figures and the events surrounding them, allowing readers to form their own informed perspectives. Through this work, I strive to foster understanding and encourage critical thinking. Thank you for joining me on this journey.

-Josephs Quartzy (Author)

About the Author

Josephs Quartzy is a Tanzanian television actor, author, and former lead vocalist for the musical duo The Eastern Bandits.

As an author, Josephs Quartzy has written books such as "*Sweetest Song I Know*," "*Irene the Andromeda*," and "*A Tale of an Intelligent Psychopath: Based on a True Story*." He is recognized for his work in fictional and philosophical novels.

Josephs Quartzy's writing career began in 2018 during his high school years, where he authored books like "*The World of Philosophy*" and "*Life's Telescope*".

Acknowledgement

I would like to express my deepest gratitude to the individuals who have been instrumental in the completion of this book.

First and foremost, I owe a debt of gratitude to myself for the unwavering determination, countless hours of hard work, and the refusal to give up, even in the face of challenges.

To my fans and clients, whose unwavering support, constructive feedback, and continued interest in my work have been the driving force behind my creative endeavors, I am profoundly thankful.

To Eliah Thomas, a brother, a devoted fan, and a trusted friend, your encouragement, insightful advice, and unwavering belief in my abilities have been invaluable throughout this journey.

To Alex Johnson, a brother and mentor, whose generous financial support and unwavering belief in my potential have enabled me to pursue my passion with greater confidence and determination.

And to Jacklin N., a remarkable individual whose steadfast support and encouragement have been a constant source of inspiration, I extend my heartfelt appreciation.

Without the support and encouragement of each of these individuals, this book would not have been possible. Thank you for believing in me and for being a part of this incredible journey.

Introduction

Welcome to the wild world of American politics, where Joe Biden and Donald Trump have strutted onto the stage like a duo in a never-ending sitcom. Picture Biden, the seasoned politician, dishing out empathy like it's candy at a parade, while Trump, the real estate tycoon turned commander-in-chief, storms in like a bull in a china shop, only to redecorate the entire place in his own style.

Their stories read like a comedy of errors, with Biden playing the straight man to Trump's erratic antics. From hobnobbing with everyday folks to Trump's larger-than-life persona that's more polarizing than pineapple on pizza, these two have turned the White House into a reality TV show where the drama never seems to end.

And oh, the controversies! From policy mishaps to personal scandals, these guys have had more ups and downs than a rollercoaster in an earthquake zone. Whether they're delivering inspiring speeches or sparking national debates with a tweet, their words have sent shockwaves across the land, leaving us all wondering what in the world is going on.

So buckle up and join us on this rollercoaster ride through the lives of Joe Biden and Donald Trump. It's a tale of power, ambition, and more plot twists than your favorite binge-worthy series. Get ready to laugh, cry, and scratch your head in disbelief as we dive deep into the absurdity of modern political history.

The Biden/Trump Rivalry Ah, the Biden/Trump rivalry, the ultimate showdown between the seasoned pro and the reality TV star turned politician. It's like watching your grandpa challenge a professional wrestler to a thumb war – equal parts amusing and bewildering. Biden, with his classic charm offensive, and Trump, with his Twitter-fueled tirades, have engaged in a battle of wits that would make even Shakespeare scratch his head in confusion.

But let's not forget the debates! Watching Biden and Trump go head-to-head on stage was like witnessing a verbal slap fight at a family reunion. Biden, with his folksy wisdom, and Trump, with his... well, whatever that was, duked it out like a couple of prizefighters in a ring made of soundbites and one-liners. It was political theater at its finest, complete with eye rolls, interruptions, and the occasional mic drop moment that left us all wondering if this was real life or just an elaborate episode of Saturday Night Live.

And what about the election drama? It was like waiting for the season finale of your favorite TV show – you knew it was coming, but you had no idea how it would all play out. From Biden's basement broadcasts to Trump's midnight Twitter rants, the race to the White House was a nail-biter of epic proportions, with enough twists and turns to make a soap opera jealous.

In the end, though, one thing is clear: the Biden/Trump rivalry will go down in history as one of the most bizarre and entertaining chapters in American politics. So grab your popcorn, folks, and settle in for the ride of a lifetime as we relive the highs, the lows, and the downright absurd moments of this unforgettable rivalry.

Who are These Fellas?

Joe Biden

born *Joseph Robinette Biden Jr.* on November 20, 1942, is an American politician who serve(s/d) as the 46th President of the United States. Before assuming the presidency, he held the position of the 47th Vice President under Barack Obama from 2009 to 2017. Additionally, Biden represented the state of Delaware in the U.S. Senate from 1973 to 2009.

I prepared some little facts about Joe Biden:

Early Life and Career:

- Biden was born in Scranton, Pennsylvania and later moved to Claymont, Delaware with his family.

- He graduated from the University of Delaware and Syracuse Law School.

- Biden served on the New Castle County Council before entering national politics.

Personal Tragedy:

- Shortly after being elected to the Senate, a devastating car accident took the lives of his wife, Neilia, and daughter, Naomi. His sons, Hunter and Beau, were critically injured.

- Biden was sworn into the Senate at his sons' hospital bedsides and continued to commute between Wilmington and Washington to be with his family.

Family and Education:

- Biden married *Jill Jacobs* in 1977. Jill is a lifelong educator and holds a doctorate in education.

- Their family was completed with the birth of their daughter, Ashley Blazer Biden.

Senate Career:

- During his 36 years in the Senate, Biden became a leader in addressing domestic and international challenges.

- As Chairman or Ranking Member of the Senate Judiciary Committee, he played a crucial role in writing and spearheading the Violence Against Women Act.

- Biden also served as Chairman or Ranking Member of the Senate Foreign Relations Committee, shaping U.S. foreign policy on various critical issues.

Vision and Values:

- Biden believes that America is an idea—one that transcends military might and guarantees dignity for all.

- His life's mission includes ending cancer, inspired by his son Beau's fight against brain cancer.

Donald Trump

Early Life and Business Ventures

Donald John Trump born June 14, 1946 is an American politician, media personality, and businessman who served as the 45th president of the United States from 2017 to 2021. His presidency was marked by various controversies and scandals.

I prepared key points about Donald Trump too:

Education: Trump received a Bachelor of Science in economics from the University of Pennsylvania in 19681.

Business Career: He was named president of his father's real estate business in 19711.

Political Affiliations: Trump has been associated with various political parties, including the Republican Party, Reform Party, Democratic Party, and Independent.

Personal Life: He has been married three times: to *Ivana Zelníčková, Marla Maples, and Melania Knavs*.

A Global Brand and Iconic Properties

Trump Tower, Mar-a-Lago, and Trump International Hotel—these iconic structures bear witness to his architectural vision. His hotels, golf courses, and resorts span the globe, attracting tourists and investors alike. Trump's brand became a symbol of luxury, elegance, and success.

The Reality TV Phenomenon

Beyond business, Trump conquered television. As the host of "The Apprentice," he mentored aspiring entrepreneurs, imparting wisdom and resilience. His catchphrase, "You're fired!", resonated with viewers, emphasizing the importance of accountability and decisiveness.

Presidential Leadership

In 2016, Trump embarked on a new chapter: the 45th President of the United States. His administration prioritized economic growth, tax reform, and deregulation.

The Ruling Systems

Joe Biden's presidency differs from Donald Trump's administration in several key ways:

Policy Priorities: Biden's policy agenda prioritizes issues like climate change, healthcare reform, immigration reform, and economic recovery. He has also emphasized unity and bipartisanship in addressing these challenges. Trump's administration focused heavily on issues like immigration enforcement, tax cuts, deregulation, and trade protectionism.

Approach to Governance: Biden has sought to govern through collaboration with Congress, stakeholders, and international allies. He has emphasized the importance of traditional institutions and norms of democracy. Trump's approach was often characterized by a more confrontational style, challenging established norms, and frequently bypassing traditional channels of governance, relying heavily on executive orders.

International Relations: Biden has taken steps to rebuild relationships with traditional allies and re-engage with international organizations such as the World Health Organization and the Paris Climate Agreement. Trump's "America First" foreign policy approach often strained relationships with allies and led to tensions with international organizations.

Tone and Rhetoric: Biden's rhetoric tends to be more measured and conciliatory, emphasizing unity and healing divisions within the country. In contrast, Trump's rhetoric was often combative, divisive, and characterized by attacks on political opponents and the media.

Response to the COVID-19 Pandemic: Biden has prioritized a science-based approach to managing the COVID-19 pandemic, emphasizing vaccine distribution, mask mandates, and economic relief measures. Trump's response was criticized for inconsistencies, downplaying the severity of the virus at times, and conflicts with public health experts.

All in all, rating on how these two leaders were good on their terms, I can say; both administrations had distinct policies, approaches, and impacts. Some people may have favored Trump's policies on issues such as tax cuts, deregulation, and foreign policy, while others appreciated Biden's emphasis on climate change, healthcare reform, and diversity and inclusion initiatives. Evaluating the effectiveness or goodness of each administration involves considering various factors, including economic performance, social progress, international relations, and overall governance. Ultimately, opinions on this matter vary widely among Americans.

Sexism, Gender & LGBTQ+ Agenda

BIDEN

Joe Biden, as a politician and public figure, has spoken out against gender discrimination and sexism throughout his career. He has advocated for policies aimed at promoting gender equality and has emphasized the importance of addressing issues such as equal pay, reproductive rights, and violence against women.During his presidential campaign in 2020, Biden frequently addressed gender equality and pledged to appoint diverse individuals, including women, to key positions within his administration. He has also expressed support for the Violence Against Women Act, which he played a significant role in passing during his time in the Senate.Additionally, Biden has been vocal about his commitment to advancing LGBTQ+ rights, including protections against discrimination based on gender identity and sexual orientation.Overall, Joe Biden's views on gender and sexism align with those of many progressive leaders, emphasizing the need for equality and the elimination of discrimination based on gender.

Lgbtq+ viewpoint

Joe Biden has been a vocal supporter of LGBTQ+ rights throughout his political career. He has consistently advocated for equal rights and protections for LGBTQ+ individuals, both legislatively and through his public statements.

Some key aspects of Biden's views on LGBTQ+ communities include:

- **Support for Marriage Equality:** Biden publicly endorsed marriage equality in 2012, becoming the highest-ranking U.S. official at the time to support same-sex marriage. He hailed the Supreme Court's decision in Obergefell v. Hodges, which legalized same-sex marriage nationwide, as a historic victory for equality.

- **Opposition to Discrimination**: Biden has spoken out against discrimination based on sexual orientation and gender identity. He supports legislation such as the Equality Act, which aims to prohibit discrimination against LGBTQ+ individuals in various areas including employment, housing, and public accommodations.

- **Transgender Rights:** Biden has voiced support for transgender rights and protections. He has condemned policies that discriminate against transgender individuals, such as the transgender military ban implemented during the Trump administration. Biden reversed this ban shortly after taking office as President.

- **Healthcare Access**: Biden has emphasized the importance of ensuring access to healthcare for LGBTQ+ individuals, including affirming the rights of transgender people to receive appropriate medical care.

TRUMP

Donald Trump's views on gender and sexism are complex and often contentious, with supporters and critics offering divergent interpretations of his words and actions.

Some aspects of Trump's views on gender and sexism include:

Controversial Statements: Trump has made numerous controversial statements about women, including derogatory remarks about their appearance and intelligence. His comments have been widely criticized as sexist and demeaning.

Allegations of Misconduct: Trump has faced multiple allegations of sexual misconduct and harassment from women over the years. These allegations have been the subject of significant media attention and controversy.

Policy Positions: During his presidency, Trump's administration took various policy positions that some critics argued were harmful to gender equality. These included rolling back protections for transgender individuals, restricting access to reproductive healthcare services, and appointing judges with conservative views on women's rights issues.

Supporters' Views: While some of Trump's supporters view him as a strong advocate for traditional gender roles and values, others have criticized his behavior and statements regarding women and gender issues.

Lgbtq+ viewpoint

While Donald Trump made some statements indicating support for LGBTQ+ rights, his administration's policies and actions often reflected more conservative positions that were perceived as harmful to LGBTQ+ individuals and communities.

Mixed Statements: During his presidential campaign in 2016, Trump presented himself as a supporter of LGBTQ+ rights, particularly in comparison to some other Republican candidates. He stated that he would be a better ally to the LGBTQ+ community than his Democratic opponent, Hillary Clinton. However, his rhetoric and policy decisions have been inconsistent on this front.

Rollbacks on LGBTQ+ Protections: Once in office, Trump's administration took several actions perceived as detrimental to LGBTQ+ rights. These included attempts to ban transgender individuals from serving in the military, rolling back protections for transgender students in schools, and supporting religious freedom exemptions that critics argued could enable discrimination against LGBTQ+ individuals.

Supreme Court Decision: In 2020, the Trump administration supported efforts to allow employers to discriminate against LGBTQ+ employees based on their sexual orientation or gender identity. However, in a landmark ruling, the Supreme Court decided that federal employment law protects LGBTQ+ workers from discrimination.

Global Perspective: The Trump administration also faced criticism for its global stance on LGBTQ+ rights. Trump's Secretary of State, Mike Pompeo, established a Commission on Unalienable Rights that some feared could undermine

LGBTQ+ rights internationally by prioritizing religious freedom over other human rights.

14	JOSEPHS QUARTZY

LGBTQ+ rights internationally by prioritizing religious freedom over other human rights.

Scandals

BIDEN

Plagiarism Accusations: In 1987, during his presidential campaign, Biden faced allegations of plagiarism related to speeches and academic work. This included accusations of lifting phrases from other politicians without proper attribution.

Anita Hill Hearings: During Supreme Court Justice Clarence Thomas's confirmation hearings in 1991, Biden, as the chairman of the Senate Judiciary Committee, faced criticism for his handling of Anita Hill's sexual harassment allegations against Thomas.

Iraq War Vote: Biden supported the resolution that authorized the invasion of Iraq in 2002, a decision that later drew criticism as the war became increasingly unpopular.

Comments on Desegregation and Busing: Biden's past comments and positions on issues related to desegregation and busing during the 1970s and 1980s have been the subject of criticism and scrutiny, particularly regarding his opposition to federally mandated busing to desegregate schools.

Allegations of Inappropriate Behavior: In 2019, several women came forward with allegations of inappropriate behavior by Biden, including instances of unwanted touching and kissing. Biden has denied any wrongdoing but acknowledged the need to be more mindful of personal space.

TRUMP

Russia Investigation: The investigation into Russian interference in the 2016 presidential election, led by Special Counsel Robert Mueller, loomed large over Trump's presidency. While the investigation did not establish conspiracy between the Trump campaign and Russia, it did outline instances of potential obstruction of justice by the president.

Impeachment: Trump was impeached twice by the House of Representatives. The first impeachment in December 2019 accused him of abuse of power and obstruction of Congress related to his dealings with Ukraine. The second impeachment in January 2021 charged him with incitement of insurrection following the Capitol riot on January 6, 2021.

Stormy Daniels Scandal: Trump faced allegations of extramarital affairs, including with adult film actress Stormy Daniels, and subsequent efforts to cover up these affairs, which led to legal battles and controversies.Family Separation Policy: Trump's administration implemented a policy of separating migrant children from their parents at the U.S.-Mexico border, which sparked widespread condemnation and legal challenges.

COVID-19 Pandemic Response: Trump's handling of the COVID-19 pandemic, including downplaying the severity of the virus, contradictory messaging, and criticism of the federal government's response, was highly controversial and polarizing.

Business and Tax Practices: Trump's business dealings and tax practices, including allegations of tax evasion and conflicts of interest related to his businesses while serving as president, were subjects of scrutiny and investigation.

Racism

Biden

Joe Biden and Donald Trump present contrasting perspectives on racism, each shaping their approach to addressing racial inequalities in America. Biden's stance is rooted in acknowledging systemic racism and proposing tangible solutions to dismantle its pervasive effects. Through initiatives like the "Biden Plan for strengthening America's Commitment to Justice," he aims to eliminate racial disparities and offer second chances to those affected by the criminal justice system. This plan includes abolishing private prisons, cash bail, and the death penalty, while also advocating for an independent task force to combat discrimination.

Trump

In contrast, Trump's track record on racism has been marred by controversies, including his promotion of the debunked "birther" conspiracy theory against President Barack Obama and his perceived mishandling of racial unrest in the nation. Despite criticism, Trump has defended himself, claiming to be the "least racist person" and highlighting economic opportunities created for African Americans during his presidency.

The divergent views between Biden and Trump on racism extend beyond policy proposals and delve into their rhetoric and behavior. Biden has openly criticized Trump's rhetoric on race, describing him as "a very nasty and vicious racist." Conversely, Trump has dismissed such accusations, asserting his commitment to racial equality while downplaying criticism of his actions.

The clash of perspectives underscores broader societal debates on racism, justice, and equality in America. While Biden advocates for proactive measures to address systemic injustices, Trump's approach is characterized by defensiveness and claims of achievement in race relations. Ultimately, the contrasting views on racism between Biden and Trump reflect deeper ideological divides within the nation, shaping the discourse on race and politics in contemporary America.

International Affairs

BIDEN

Afghanistan: The Biden administration oversaw the withdrawal of U.S. troops from Afghanistan, ending America's longest war. However, the withdrawal was criticized for its chaotic nature and the subsequent takeover of the country by the Taliban.

China: Relations between the U.S. and China remained tense during the Biden administration, with issues such as trade, technology, human rights, and territorial disputes in the South China Sea being major points of contention.

Russia: The relationship between the U.S. and Russia remained strained, with disputes over election interference, cyberattacks, human rights abuses, and territorial conflicts like Ukraine and Crimea.

Iran: The Biden administration sought to revive the Iran nuclear deal (Joint Comprehensive Plan of Action or JCPOA), negotiating with Iran and other signatories to return to compliance with the agreement. However, negotiations faced challenges, and tensions persisted over Iran's nuclear program.

North Korea: Efforts to engage with North Korea were limited, with North Korea conducting missile tests and showing little willingness to engage in meaningful dialogue on denuclearization.

European Union: The Biden administration sought to repair and strengthen transatlantic ties, focusing on issues such as climate change, trade, and security cooperation.

Middle East: The administration maintained support for Israel while also seeking to revive peace talks between Israelis and Palestinians. It also engaged with regional allies and partners to address conflicts and stabilize the region.

TRUMP

China: The Trump administration engaged in a trade war with China, imposing tariffs on Chinese goods and pursuing a more confrontational approach to address issues such as intellectual property theft, trade imbalances, and technology transfer.

Russia: Despite allegations of Russian interference in the 2016 U.S. presidential election, President Trump pursued a somewhat conciliatory approach toward Russia, often expressing a desire for improved relations. However, tensions persisted over issues such as election interference, sanctions, and conflicts in Ukraine and Syria.

North Korea: President Trump engaged in unprecedented diplomacy with North Korean leader Kim Jong-un, including multiple summits and personal meetings. While these efforts led to a temporary easing of tensions and symbolic gestures, such as the suspension of missile tests, substantive progress toward denuclearization remained elusive.

European Union: The Trump administration had a contentious relationship with the European Union, marked by disputes over trade, NATO contributions, climate change, and Iran nuclear deal.

Middle East: The Trump administration pursued a series of policies in the Middle East, including moving the U.S. embassy in Israel to Jerusalem, brokering normalization agreements between Israel and some Arab states, and withdrawing from the Iran nuclear deal.

Mexico: President Trump's signature campaign promise was the construction of a border wall between the U.S. and Mexico, which led to strained relations between the two countries. Tensions also arose over trade negotiations and immigration policies.

Wealthy

Biden

President Joe Biden's financial standing has garnered attention, particularly due to his extensive tenure in public office. Despite referring to himself as "the poorest man in Congress," Biden's net worth has experienced fluctuations over time. As of 2024, his financial status is influenced by various factors:

Source of Income: Biden has derived income from avenues such as book deals and speaking engagements, experiencing notable increases particularly during the Trump administration.

Possessions: While specific details about Biden's assets remain largely undisclosed, his financial situation reflects earnings accumulated through public service and other endeavors.

Controversies: Though Biden's wealth hasn't been a focal point of contention, scrutiny has surrounded his financial disclosures and income sources, with attention given to matters of transparency and potential conflicts of interest.

Trump

Former President Donald Trump is renowned for his extensive business empire and real estate ventures, which have significantly molded his financial profile. Here are key insights regarding Trump's wealth:

Source of Income: Trump's primary wealth stems from his vast real estate holdings, business ventures, and investment endeavors. His net worth has been subject to speculation and scrutiny over the years.

Possessions: Trump possesses various properties, including upscale estates, golf courses, and commercial buildings, reflecting his stature as a prominent figure in the business arena.

Controversies: Trump's wealth has been mired in controversies concerning tax practices, business transactions, and potential conflicts of interest during his presidency. His financial disclosures and business decisions have often sparked debates and investigations.

In essence, both Joe Biden and Donald Trump boast distinctive financial backgrounds shaped by their respective careers, investments, and public personas. While Biden's wealth has witnessed fluctuations linked to his political journey and supplementary income streams like books and speeches, Trump's riches are deeply intertwined with his expansive real estate holdings and entrepreneurial pursuits. The controversies encircling their finances underscore the intricacies of financial transparency and responsibility within the spheres of politics and business.

Controversial Decisions

Some of the most controversial decisions made by Joe Biden and Donald Trump during their presidency include:

Biden

Big spending: Biden proposed a $3 trillion plan that aimed to expand social safety net programs and make significant investments in education and housing, which was criticized as a risky move during the pandemic

Afghanistan withdrawal: Biden's decision to withdraw troops from Afghanistan was met with criticism, as it was seen as a hasty and uncoordinated move that left many Americans and Afghan allies behind

Call with Xi Jinping: Biden's call with his Chinese counterpart Xi Jinping was seen as a tense moment in US-China relations, with Biden raising concerns about China's economic practices and human rights abuses

Protecting abortion access: Biden made protecting abortion access a central campaign theme in the 2022 midterm elections, which was a divisive issue among voters

Deficit reduction: Biden's efforts to reduce the deficit through tax increases and spending cuts were criticized by some Democrats who felt they were too aggressive

Trump

Tax cuts: Trump signed a $1.5 trillion tax cut package in 2017, which was criticized for being heavily skewed towards the wealthy and for adding to the federal deficit

Health care overhaul: Trump's efforts to repeal and replace the Affordable Care Act were met with significant opposition and failed to pass

Obstruction of justice: Trump was accused of obstructing justice during the Mueller investigation into Russian interference in the 2016 election

Immigration policies: Trump's hardline immigration policies, including the separation of families at the border and the travel ban, were widely criticized.

Trade policies: Trump's trade policies, including tariffs on China and renegotiation of NAFTA, were seen as disruptive to global trade and led to retaliatory measures from other countries

Presidential Legacies

BIDEN

During Joe's tenure as Vice President of the United States under President Barack Obama from 2009 to 2017. During this time, he played a significant role in shaping U.S. domestic and foreign policies, including the Affordable Care Act (Obamacare), economic recovery efforts following the 2008 financial crisis, and various diplomatic initiatives.

Before his vice presidency, Biden served as a United States Senator from Delaware for over three decades, from 1973 to 2009. As a senator, he chaired the Senate Judiciary Committee and the Senate Foreign Relations Committee, where he contributed to legislation on crime, foreign affairs, and other key issues.

TRUMP

During his presidency, he implemented several policies and initiatives, including:

Tax cuts and reforms (Tax Cuts and Jobs Act of 2017)

Efforts to repeal and replace the Affordable Care Act (Obamacare)

Immigration policies, including the travel ban targeting several predominantly Muslim countries

Trade policies, renegotiating trade deals such as the North American Free Trade Agreement (NAFTA) and imposing tariffs on imports, particularly from China

Nominations of conservative judges, including three Supreme Court justices

Foreign policy decisions, such as withdrawing from the Iran nuclear deal and the Paris Climate Agreement

Negotiations with North Korea over its nuclear program

Socialization

TRUMP

Donald Trump's social life has been widely covered in the media due to his high-profile status as a businessman, television personality, and politician. Here are some aspects of his social life:

Celebrity Connections: Trump has had connections with various celebrities and public figures over the years, both through his business ventures and his involvement in the entertainment industry. He has appeared in numerous television shows, movies, and interviews, often interacting with celebrities from different fields.

Social Events and Galas: Trump has been known to attend and host high-profile social events, including galas, fundraisers, and charity functions. He has also been a prominent figure in the New York City social scene, attending parties and gatherings with other influential individuals.

Membership in Exclusive Clubs: Trump has been associated with exclusive clubs and organizations, including golf clubs and private resorts, where he socializes with other members of the affluent community.

Use of Social Media: Trump has been an avid user of social media platforms, where he has shared his thoughts, opinions, and announcements with millions of followers. His use of socials has often generated controversy and garnered significant attention.

Overall, Trump's social life reflects his status as a prominent public figure with connections across various industries and circles. His interactions and relationships have been closely scrutinized, given his role in politics and his presence in the media spotlight.

BIDEN

Biden and his team have utilized social media platforms to engage with supporters, share campaign updates, and communicate his policy positions. While not as prolific as some other politicians on social media, Biden has recognized its importance as a tool for outreach and connection.

Famous Quotations

Here are ten quotes attributed to Joe Biden:

"We are the United States of America. There is not a single thing we cannot do if we do it together."

"Don't tell me what you value, show me your budget, and I'll tell you what you value."

"We choose hope over fear, unity over division, science over fiction, and yes, truth over lies."

"Our future cannot depend on the government alone. The ultimate solutions lie in the attitudes and the actions of the American people."

"The American people have never, ever, ever, ever let their country down."

"Failure at some point in your life is inevitable, but giving up is unforgivable."

"Character is destiny."

"We have to do more than just give people a square deal; we have to give them a fair shot."

"Everyone is your equal, and everyone is equal to you."

"There is nothing special about being vice president. Nothing at all."

Quotes attributed to Donald Trump:

"Make America Great Again!"

"We will build a great wall along the southern border."

"You're fired!"

"I think the only difference between me and the other candidates is that I'm more honest and my women are more beautiful."

"I will be the greatest jobs president that God ever created."

"I'm really rich."

"When somebody challenges you, fight back. Be brutal, be tough."

"The point is, you can never be too greedy."

"I love the poorly educated."

"I have great respect for women. Nobody has more respect for women than I do."

What People Wants

Trump

Voters generally feel colder about Donald Trump than they do about Joe Biden. When asked to rate the two candidates on a "feeling thermometer," where 0 is the coldest rating and 100 is the warmest rating:

51% of registered voters give Trump a "very cold" rating of less than 25 (including 40% who give him a zero – the lowest possible rating).

38% give Biden a "very cold" rating (including 25% who give him a zero rating).

There is a more modest gap in the shares expressing "warm" or "very warm" feelings:

43% give Biden a rating over 50, compared with 38% who give Trump a warm rating.

Among Trump supporters, 68% have very warm feelings toward the former president, while about half of Biden's voters (52%) feel similarly warm toward him.

Negative views of the other party's candidate:

Nine-in-ten Biden supporters give Trump a very cold rating (including fully 73% who give him the lowest possible rating – zero).

By comparison, 79% of Trump voters give Biden a very cold rating (with 55% rating him at 0).

Overall, voters give Biden an average rating of 45 on the 100-point scale compared with Trump's score of 39.

Women tend to give Trump substantially lower ratings than Biden.

Older voters are more likely to give Trump a warmer rating than younger voters.

Educational divides in ratings are widest among those with a college degree or more.

Biden

About four-in-ten Americans (37%) approve of Joe Biden's job performance as president, while 60% disapprove. His approval rating remains relatively unchanged from earlier in the summer and is far lower than it was in the early months of his presidency.

In summary, opinions on both Trump and Biden vary significantly, reflecting the political polarization in the United States.

Sworn Enemies

Donald Trump and Joe Biden have faced different adversaries during their political careers:

Trump

Joe Biden: Trump's political rival and opponent in the 2020 presidential election. Their contentious relationship continues to shape American politics.

Former South Carolina Gov. Nikki Haley: Competed against Trump in the Republican presidential primary. Haley represents the pre-Trump GOP, making her a perfect foil for Trump.

Democrats: As a Republican president, Trump faced opposition from the Democratic Party, including Democratic lawmakers in Congress who often opposed his policies and legislative initiatives.

Media Outlets: Trump frequently clashed with various media outlets, particularly those he labeled as "fake news" for their critical coverage of his administration.

Deep State Allegations: Trump often spoke about a "deep state" within the government bureaucracy, suggesting that there were entrenched interests working against him from within the federal government.

Global Leaders: Trump's foreign policy decisions and diplomatic style sometimes put him at odds with leaders of other countries, including traditional allies like Germany and Canada.

Biden

Donald Trump: Biden has criticized Trump's extreme MAGA Republicans, considering them a threat to American democracy

.

MAGA Republicans: Biden warns that they represent an extremism that endangers the foundations of the republic.

In the complex world of politics, these figures clash, each with their own strengths and weaknesses.

Republicans in Congress: Biden faces significant opposition from Republican lawmakers in Congress, particularly in passing key pieces of legislation and advancing his policy agenda.

Conservative Media: Similar to Trump, Biden has faced criticism from conservative media outlets that oppose his policies and question his leadership.

Progressive Wing of the Democratic Party: While Biden is a centrist figure, he has faced criticism from the more progressive wing of the Democratic Party, particularly on issues such as healthcare, climate change, and economic policy.

Foreign Adversaries: As President, Biden has to navigate complex relationships with adversarial countries such as Russia,

China, Iran, and North Korea, which pose challenges to U.S. interests and global stability.

Supporters, Allies and Close Friends

Trump

Supporters:

Republican Party: Trump's base includes Republican voters, elected officials, and conservative activists.

Conservative Media: Influential media personalities, such as Sean Hannity and Tucker Carlson, support Trump.

Evangelical Christians: Many evangelical Christians appreciate Trump's policies on religious freedom and pro-life issues.

National Rifle Association (NRA): The NRA and gun rights advocates back Trump.

Business Leaders: Some business leaders appreciate Trump's deregulation and tax policies.

Populist Movements: Trump's appeal extends to populist movements across the country.

Allies:

Mike Pence: As Vice President during Trump's term, Pence was a loyal ally.

Lindsey Graham: Senator Lindsey Graham has consistently supported Trump's agenda.

Rudy Giuliani: Trump's personal attorney and former New York City mayor remains a close ally.

Stephen Miller: A policy advisor, Miller played a significant role in shaping Trump's immigration policies.

Close Friends:

Ivanka Trump: Trump's daughter and advisor shares a close bond with him.

Jared Kushner: Ivanka's husband, Kushner, served as a senior advisor in the Trump administration.

Sean Hannity: The Fox News host is a personal friend and vocal supporter of Trump.

Roger Stone: A longtime associate, Stone has been a confidant to Trump.

Joe Biden and Donald Trump, both prominent figures in American politics, have distinct circles of supporters, allies, and close friends. Let's delve into their networks:

Biden

Supporters:

Democratic Party: Joe Biden enjoys strong backing from the Democratic Party, including elected officials, activists, and voters who align with its policies and values.

Progressive Groups: Progressive organizations, such as MoveOn.org and Indivisible, support Biden's agenda.

Labor Unions: Biden has garnered support from labor unions, which advocate for workers' rights and fair wages.

Civil Rights Leaders: Prominent civil rights activists and leaders endorse Biden's commitment to social justice and equality.

Young Voters: Many young voters rallied behind Biden during the 2020 election.

International Allies: Leaders of allied nations, such as European heads of state, express support for Biden's diplomatic approach.

Allies:

Kamala Harris: As Vice President, Kamala Harris is a close ally of Biden, working closely on policy initiatives.

Nancy Pelosi: The Speaker of the House, Nancy Pelosi, supports Biden's legislative agenda.

John Kerry: Former Secretary of State John Kerry is an ally, especially on climate change issues.

Barack Obama: The former President remains a trusted confidant and supporter of Biden.

Close Friends:

Jill Biden: Joe's wife, Jill Biden, is not only his partner but also a trusted advisor.

Ted Kaufman: A longtime friend and former chief of staff, Kaufman played a key role during Biden's transition to the presidency.

Cedric Richmond: As a senior advisor, Richmond is a close friend and confidant to Biden.

Steve Ricchetti: A longtime associate, Ricchetti serves as a counselor to the President.

Foreign Policies & War initiatives

Biden

Ending *"Forever Wars"*:

President Biden promised to end "forever wars" and reassert American leadership to combat authoritarianism and global instability.

He aimed to stand for values that unite democracies and address the proliferation of these challenges under Trump's presidency.

Military Strikes:

In Biden's first year, U.S. military strikes fell by 54% compared to Trump's last year in office.

Most of these strikes occurred in Afghanistan before U.S. forces withdrew in August.

Airstrikes also decreased significantly in Somalia, Iraq, and Syria due to the military defeat of the Islamic State.

Trump

War Powers Legacy:

During Trump's term in office, his war powers reporting to Congress revealed an extraordinarily broad vision of the president's authority to use force abroad without congressional authorization.

Trump exploited loopholes in reporting requirements, which obscured information on the use of force from the public.

The War Powers Resolution of 1973 (WPR), which requires consultation with Congress before introducing armed forces into hostilities, did not empower Congress to fulfill its constitutional role in deciding on matters of war and peace.

Transparency-forcing reporting requirements became the most practically useful aspect of the WPR.

Specific Actions:

Notably, Trump governed for four years without initiating any new wars.

Both presidents had distinct approaches to war powers and foreign policy, with Trump emphasizing restraint in initiating new conflicts, and Biden focusing on ending prolonged military engagements.

My ViewPoint & Where I Stand

The Two Sides of the American Coin

My Perspective on Joe Biden|Donald Trump rivalry............

In the annals of American history, the names Joe Biden and Donald Trump resonate as powerful symbols of leadership, each embodying distinct ideologies and policies that have shaped the nation's course. As a non-American citizen observing from afar, I find myself drawn to the multifaceted personas of these two remarkable individuals, recognizing their strengths and contributions from diverse vantage points.

Joe Biden, with his decades-long political career, epitomizes a seasoned statesman, steeped in the traditions of diplomacy and consensus-building. His approach to governance reflects a commitment to inclusivity and empathy, rooted in a belief in the power of dialogue and cooperation. As President, Biden has championed policies aimed at addressing pressing societal challenges, from healthcare reform to climate change mitigation, seeking to forge a path towards a more equitable and sustainable future.

On the other side of the coin stands Donald Trump, a figure whose unconventional style and unapologetic rhetoric have left an indelible mark on the American political landscape. Trump's presidency was marked by a fervent commitment to populist ideals and a bold, America-first agenda. His unabashed nationalism resonated deeply with a significant portion of the electorate, as he promised to prioritize the interests of the

American people above all else. Through his policies on trade, immigration, and national security, Trump sought to redefine America's role in the global arena, challenging conventional wisdom and sparking passionate debate.

While Biden and Trump may appear diametrically opposed in their approaches to governance, they represent complementary facets of the American experience, each contributing unique insights and perspectives to the national dialogue. Biden's pragmatism and emphasis on consensus-building serve as a counterbalance to Trump's boldness and unwavering conviction. Together, they form the yin and yang of American politics, embodying the enduring tension between tradition and innovation, unity and division.

In the grand tapestry of American history, the contributions of Biden and Trump serve as a testament to the resilience of democracy and the enduring spirit of the American people. While their legacies may be subject to interpretation and debate, there can be no denying the profound impact they have had on the course of the nation's history. As we look towards the future, it is imperative that we draw upon the lessons of their leadership, seeking common ground and shared purpose in the pursuit of a more perfect union.

In conclusion, Joe Biden and Donald Trump represent the two sides of a coin, each essential in their own right to the rich tapestry of American democracy. As we navigate the challenges of the 21st century, let us embrace the diversity of perspectives they embody, recognizing that true progress lies in our ability to learn from the past and chart a course towards a brighter tomorrow.

Don't miss out!

Visit the website below and you can sign up to receive emails whenever Josephs Quartzy publishes a new book. There's no charge and no obligation.

https://books2read.com/r/B-A-YNVV-VJQYC

BOOKS2READ

Connecting independent readers to independent writers.

Did you love *The Chase: Trump Vs Biden*? Then you should read *A Blessed Curse*[1] by Josephs Quartzy!

[2]

A revised version of A Blessed Curse potraying Suzanne Bowman left alone as an orphan at the age of 10 when her parents where burned to death accused of witchcraft, no one ever wanted her or near her kids but a servant's daughter Mali became her first family. Sergeant Alexander O'shea sent in Africa met Suzzy as an evangelist, they became friends because O'shea loved her african friend (Nilindiwe). Young Nlindiwe who was in love with O'shea is Married to Upare's chief Maludkwa as a 10th wife,

---

1. https://books2read.com/u/bMxMZX

2. https://books2read.com/u/bMxMZX

she gets pregnant but a biracial child is born, Chief Maludkwa is angry with her and plans to kill her because she cheated him.

Also by Josephs Quartzy

A Blessed Curse
A Blessed Curse

Proven Laws of Life
Proven Laws of Life You Must Know

Standalone
Love or Medicine
Philosophies From an Old Journal
Sweetest Song I Know
Race and Changes
The Chase: Trump Vs Biden

About the Publisher

Bongo Times Now is a Media company and publisher from Tanzania founded in 2019

www.ingramcontent.com/pod-product-compliance
Lightning Source LLC
Chambersburg PA
CBHW051816130726
47987CB00003B/1280